T0167111

CHERRIES ON THE CAKE

D. ANNE AUSTIN

 www.trafford.com
North America & international
toll-free: 1 888 232 4444 (USA & Canada)
fax: 812 355 4082

For my family and friends, worldwide

Cherry blossoms
Waving softly in the wind,
And their exuberant children
Cherries, scarlet and fat
Glistening with joy

D. Anne Austin

SCOTLAND

Well, maybe I am an International Clairvoyant / Medium, but am also a woman who loves to cook and I thought it might be entertaining to share with u, my travels and include recipes from that place, that time, in my life. So this will be a chronological journey as well as a gastronomic one.

Scotland, my place of birth, is a land of great beauty, of majestic mountains, of peaceful lochs and a climate of cold winters and winds that cut through to the bone!

Aberdeenshire, bringing in the New Year, walking along the farm track with painfully cold knees and Edinburgh, as a student, climbing up Waverley steps, are memories of extreme discomfort in wintertime. So, of course, my mind turns to soup! That wonderfully life sustaining, nourishing and comforting food which every country and culture hold in high esteem. Many top chefs maintain that in the making of soup and sauces, the true genius is found. Now that is certainly not me, but making soup is my favourite dish. Nothing nicer than seeing family returning home, red nosed and shivering, eyes lighting up as they inhale the aroma of the soup pot, pulling up their chairs and drinking their soup with relish! (Homemade bread as well.)

That sounds like I made good bread. Not so! If it looked good, the taste suffered.

If it fell to pieces it was much tastier, though it was often referred to as 'elephants' feet.'

At a rugby ball in the Borders, I was dancing with a rugby playing chef who had just won a Michelin star for his French onion soup. He kindly gave me the recipe as we danced.

French Onion Soup

Ingredients:

2 PINTS OF BEEF STOCK MADE BY SIMMERING SHIN BEEF
4LARGE WHITE ONIONS SLICED ACROSS INTO RINGS
3 OUNCES OF BUTTER
1 TEASPOONFUL OF CASTOR SUGAR
1 SMALL WINEGLASSFUL OF DRY SHERRY
SALT AND BLACK PEPPER
GRATED CHEESE AND CROUTONS TO SERVE ALONGSIDE

Instructions:

1. MELT THE BUTTER, FRY THE ONIONS TILL GOLDEN BROWN.
2. ADD THE SUGAR, STIRRING. WITH SEASONING.
3. NEXT THE BEEF STOCK, LASTLY THE SHERRY,
4. SIMMER FOR 20 MINUTES.

5. HAND THE CHEESE AND CROUTON SEPARATELY

I wonder if he remembers the dance and the conversation. He, in his kilt, me, in my favourite soft, black, Spanish style, long muslin, dress with tiny gold dots. How evocative the memory of clothes can be!

My godmother told me about her first ball which she attended with my mother. She, indelicate pale blue tulle and my mother in red velvet with a square neckline who choked trying to smoke her first cigarette.

We had a large Victorian house in Scotland and grew vegetables in the back garden. There was a large stone built outhouse with lots of room for my wine making, collecting dandelions, hawthorn berries, elderflowers from our walks along the old railway line. The best of the wines was undoubtedly peapod wine. Dry, and excellent with fish. You discard or cook the peas and use the skins only. Dandelion was a gorgeous, bright golden, yellow wine and a great pick me up, excellent for the heart.

Autumn is a favourite season, probably because I was born at the end of September, and, according to my mother, a joyful child always.

Scotland is glorious in Autumn, with the red rowan trees, walking in the woods, crunching through the leaves, seeing all the rich tints and shades of the different species of tree.

All animal lovers, we had our animal family, Barney, the crazy lovable mixed pedigree dog who ate the minister's chickens and whose friend

Shift, a Dachshund, came for him daily to make mischief. No matter how careful we were in closing the sliding wooden door to the garden to stop the escape, in the melee of getting four children and two adults out for school, they would sprint off.

Our house had been a guest house for the annual Game Fair

Before this we had lived in a tiny village in a schoolhouse in the Scottish Borders which was really haunted by a young soldier who had once lived there.

Our older son was studying bagpipes and needed a set of his own.

He had studied the violin also but preferred the bagpipes.

We had searched all of the likely places for a set and were almost giving up hope, when we found a set in a local newspaper.

Ebony, ivory and silver. Very expensive!

It seemed like a plan to run the house as a guest house for a few days, when the income would cover the cost of the bagpipes. So when people phoned. I booked them in. Seventeen in all. The judges at the Fair had to have early breakfast, 5.30am, next shift 6.30am and so on. Keeping the bacon unburned was a major worry! I had said only breakfast. but some were coming from the south of England so prepared evening meals as well.

Handwrote the menus,. and prepared soup and chicken and syllabub.

After the meal, one of the guests hung back. I immediately worried what might be wrong with the food.

"I loved the soup. Please may I have the recipe?'

Could have hugged her!

Without the help of my older daughter aged 11, could never have done it.

And the bagpipes were borne in, in triumph!

Cream of Lettuce Soup

Ingredients:

2 OLD LETTUCES (USE UP FROM GARDEN)
2 OZ'S BUTTER
1 OZ FLOUR
SALT AND PEPPER
2 ONIONS
1 SPRING ONION
CHICKEN STOCK
A LITTLE CREAM

Instructions:

1. MELT THE BUTTER ADD THE FLOUR
2. LITTLE BY LITTLE, ADD THE STOCK
3. PUT THE ROUGHLY CHOPPED, WASHED, LETTUCE INTO THE MIXTURE.
4. ADD BLENDED ONIONS
5. SIMMER AND ADD SEASONING
6. FINALLY A SWIRL OF CREAM JUST BEFORE SERVING
7. GARNISH WITH WATERCRESS.

Dinner parties were very much a focus of life then, as were balls, squash club dances and parties of course. The Halloween party for the children and friends was the favourite. Wearing oldest clothes, not to get in a mess, playing the traditional games, such as dooking for apples with a fork between the teeth and eating treacle scones, suspended from a pulley, followed by scary Halloween stories, we loved it all!

When there was a dinner party, the children all ate early. Between courses there would be a 'psst' from the children on each floor, looking for left -overs and specially syllabub, a Medieval pudding which I always prepared the night before.

So simple, so good!

Syllabub

Ingredients:

1 PINT OF CREAM
JUICE OF 2 LEMONS
HALF A POUND OF ICING SUGAR
1 GLASS OF SHERRY (OR U CAN USE WHITE
WINE)

Instructions:

WHISK CREAM TILL STIFF, ADD SUGAR,
SHERRY, THEN LEMON
POUR INTO WINE GLASSES AND SERVE,
AFTER A FEW HOURS
WHEN IT THICKENS, WITH A SPICY BISCUIT.

We had a crisis one Christmas Eve. The turkey was
cooling in the Raeburn.

The stuffing, both kinds made, one sage and onion, one
oatmeal stuffing,

The vegetables all prepared and the mince meat pies all baked that day, for the children and their friends had eaten the previous batch.

As well as Barney we had four very characterful cats. Domino, gracious as a butler, welcoming guests, tail held high, as he led them up the path.

Aphrodite, well named after the goddess of love, a black and white half

Persian; long haired, had produced most of the kittens in the area and beyond. Every time we took her to the vet, she was already pregnant.

Dylan had a bit of Siamese in his pedigree and was trouble!

Murphy was the gentlest of cats, a large tabby tom. His favourite foods were cucumber and mushrooms which he ate very daintily indeed.

Dylan hated him with a passion.

That Christmas Eve, a rerun of the classic film, "The Quiet Man" was on TV.

My husband, a sports fanatic, called everyone in to the sitting room to watch the fight scene. Younger daughter, who had been checking the turkey, left the oven door ajar and Dylan had the feast of his life. His sides were almost touching the floor. I was in tears of exhaustion, after the second rerun of the mince meat pies. And we had salmon that Christmas that a friend had given us to keep for him in the chest freezer. Not sure where he had come by it!

Skirlie or Oatmeal Stuffing

Ingredients:

1 LARGE ONION FINELY CHOPPED
6OZS PIN HEAD OATMEAL
SALT AND BLACK PEPPER
3 OZS LARD OR COOKING OIL

Instructions:

1. FRY THE ONIONS
2. ADD 6 OZ'S OATMEAL STIR TILL COOKED
   SEASON

GOOD REPLACEMENT FOR POTATOES; HEALTHY, FULL OF IRON

When the Scots left the Highlands and Islands to go and study in Edinburgh. They were very poor and lived away from home for a year at a time. So they carried sacks of oatmeal on their ponies, food for the year' (They also made candles to study by, using rushes, peeled, only one strip of green left, with lard poured over.)

The oatmeal would become porridge, oatcakes, brose; skirlie. The iron would sustain life but how monotonous!

As a student my father worked in his holidays on farms in Perthshire. He described the food the farmer's wife would make for the farm hands thus.

"She would make a huge pot of porridge for the week, pour it into a special drawer to set and cut squares throughout the week Not even heated. Like glue."

In Aberdeenshire, my mother in law had a meal kist which was necessary in wintertime as was the barrel of salted herrings. They could be snowed in for weeks at a time. Eggs and chicken, butter and cheese were always available.

She made her own cheese in the dairy and churned the butter. She was a truly good cook. The Women's Institute was the highlight of the week and winning prizes for the best jam or cakes made life rewarding.

Fried Herrings or Trout

CLEAN AND BONE EACH HERRING
SPRINKLE WITH SALT AND PEPPER
TOSS IN OATMEAL TILL WELL COATED
FRY IN SHALLOW FAT TILL WELL BROWNED

ENGLAND

Merstham is a beautiful small village in Surrey. The village school is Victorian with turrets and spires. On my way to an interview there, I saw the sun dance in the sky. It took my breath away. It literally danced. I wasn't thinking of spiritual things but the interview. It danced as I stood, spellbound, one of the most joyful sights I've ever experienced.

The village's claim to fame is that the Colman mustard family have lived there and drove a mustard coloured coach to the station daily, to London. Apparently the wealth comes from the mustard left on the side of the plate!.

One of my colleagues there gave me this recipe from the previous Head Teacher and it is a family favourite for all occasions.

Mackerel Pate

Ingredients:

1PACKET OF PHILADELPHIA CREAM CHEESE
(ORIGINAL)
1PACKETOF MACKEREL FILLETS SPICED
WITH BLACK PEPPER
1 LEMON, SQUEEZED

Instructions:

1. MASH THE FISH ROUGHLY. ADD THE
   CHEESE. MIX WELL.
2. ADD THE LEMON JUICE AND
   LEAVE FOR A FEW HOURS FOR THE
   FLAVOURS TO COMBINE.
3. SERVE WITH CRISPS, PITTA BREAD OR
   COCKTAIL BISCUITS

GERMANY

A major shift now to Germany and the military. An interview at Eltham Palace with majors, wing commanders, education chiefs about ten of them and myself, for a Language Post holder position. A major asked me what was my religion. I replied that that was my business only.

'Well that's that,' I thought, 'no way I'll get this job.' The faces of the panel showed shock and amusement in equal measure.

A few days later the acceptance letter came. Younger two children came with me, the older two studying in London.

My husband, waiting to go to Saudi and he would join me in Germany for his leave. We had tried for years to get a joint appointment but Fate decreed otherwise. I love the expression, "Man proposes, God Disposes!"

Those two and a half years in Germany were great in one way. The village feasts and customs. The maypole and dancing round it. The plates smashed at prewedding parties so there would be no bad luck for the young couple. The Wandern Gruppe, hiking into the countryside with fellow walkers, with their assorted dogs. They would lie, under the tables waiting expectantly, while we were having lunch in a restaurant. Amusing when they got annoyed with each other!

A scene stays in my mind so clearly from one of these walks. It was a glorious spring day, bright sunshine, wild flowers everywhere, the trees all tender green leaves. Bird singing. There was a field to our left with young horses, manes glistening in the sun, silvery like spun silk, blowing in the wind. They were a small Swedish breed, Half lingers, found also in the Orkneys and in Skyros, Greece. Their coats a delicate pale fawn, their manes and tails, silver. They galloped away, the small herd. There was not sound from the walkers or the dogs. You could have heard a pin drop. We were all transfixed by the beauty. Unforgettable.

After a car accident in London, young daughter was in a wheelchair for eighteen months while her two broken legs healed. The kindness of the Germans, mostly miners, we will never forget. So even in adversity, there can also be fun.

Herring Salat

I watched this made in Germany when the herrings from the fish market were in a bucket of water. The water had to be changed every four hours. I use a jar already prepared.

Serve with brown bread. This dish was traditionally made on New Year's Eve.

Ingredients:

1 JAR OF ROLLMOPS (HERRING IN BRINE, ROLLED U
1ONION FINELY CHOPPED
1 APPLE FINELY CHOPPED
NO SALT
1 HARDBOILED EGG CHOPPED
1 GHERKIN CHOPPED
1 TABLESPOONFUL OF CAPERS
2 SMALL COOKED BEETROOT CHOPPED
BLACK PEPPER
2 TABLE SPOONS MAYONNAISE

COMBINE. LEAVE FOR A COUPLE OF HOURS.

Potato Salad

COOKED BOILED POTATOES

1 CHOPPED RED APPLE
FRANFURTER SAUSAGES THINLY SLICED
MAYONNAISE
1SPRING ONION FINELY SLICED
SALT AND PEPPER

COMBINE

Summer Fruit Punch

Garden parties often had punch. Here is a very pleasant one.

A PRETTY JUG
1 QUARTER BOTTLE OF SCHNAPPS
I BOTTLE SWEET WHITE WINE(OR DRY)

ADD THINLY SLICED BANANAS
KIWI FRUIT SLICED AND STRAWBERRIES.

That was life in the village and then there was the Officers' Mess Oktober Fest, Annual Cocktail Party, Summer Ball and all that goes with Military life. I liked to hear the Phantoms flying over the Base. I learned a lot about life and the stresses on the families of the Military.

BOURNEMOUTH UK

Next destination, Brunei, a small country on the island of Borneo. But before that, I had to do an accelerated T.E.F.L course, Teaching English as a Foreign Language in Bournemouth.

Wow! was that tough! It was emotionally demanding, emotionally taxing. The pace was fast and furious. The director of the language school met me for coffee when I got there. He said,' This course can not be done if u are going through a divorce or a break up."

I told him my father had just died the previous week. He nodded his head.

'You can do it'

I'll never forget seeing a strong farmer on the course, crying in a graveyard in our lunch hour. Everyone was stressed out for six weeks, the duration of the course. In the first lecture there was an interactive game. It began thus:

'I am Andy and I like apples.'

'I am Andy I like apples I am Steven and I like sugar.'

'I am Andy I like apples, I am Steven and I like sugar I am Tommy and I like tomatoes.

Well I was about number 17 in the circle, and had been busy. Memorizing everyone that had gone before, all 16.My mind froze, could not think of a word for something! Anything at all! Everyone was looking down at their feet, whispering suggestions to me which I was not going to use. Eventually a word came, mortifying. But the lecturer told me to come out and write the first word that came into my mind

Stone 'Write one above.'

Heart 'Write one above'

Well 'Sit down. I know how your mind works.'

I was lucky, I think, for here was an Anglo Spanish guy, very strict, but who had a mind like mine. He told me soon as I got to Brunei to do the Diploma as well. A further year of study but it was therapeutic and I passed, (no distinction or anything.) The leader of the course said" Hardest working student we have ever had!"

The humiliation of that first game was the dynamic that drove me! Right out of the comfort zone!

BRUNEI

From the Military, orders and uniforms, (civilians didn't wear them,) but admittedly, the dress uniforms of the army, particularly, outshone the women's lovely ball gowns which the majority of the women flew to London to buy. The red stripe down the trouser leg against the black uniform had real impact. As a young child in Scotland we had to colour in outfits; boots, skirts, jackets and mine were always black and red. A vivid memory and red is still my favourite colour.

A symbol of life, courage, passion, speed and living in the moment. Like a poppy that springs up overnight. Or cherries hung from the ear to make pretty earrings!

If I think of Scotland in terms of colour it is grey and muted purples, like the lovely, soft, misty tones of woollens and tweeds.

Brunei shone in Technicolor. The baju kurongs, the traditional dress of the women were richly ornamented with embroidery and sequins. The colours, apple green, peach, scarlet, royal blue, singing pink, emerald turquoise, with matching headscarves. They were all so pretty in their satin and silks and of course their gold! Necklaces, bracelets, rings, earrings, 23 carat gold.

Sometimes I would sit back in the staffroom and just listen to a discussion about the price of gold or which currency was best to buy and I would grin a little, contrasting it to Scotland!

The men were colourfully dressed also in silk tunics with a mandarin collar and a dark, velvet songkok on their heads. This was a little like a larger version of a pillbox hat. It was a very dignified form of dress. We had to wear clothes which suited the culture of course, with longish sleeves and almost full length. Nothing transparent or immodest. The dressmaker I used got very cross eventually, for I stuck to one pattern.

'I am so tired of this,' she would say. 'can't you choose another pattern?'

The school was on the Water Village Many centuries ago the people believed in Animism, that the waterfall had a spirit, and the jungle had spirits residing there, often in stands of bamboo. So, knowing that spirits won't cross running water, they built their houses of wood, on stilts, on the river. Hospitals, schools and clinics are there to serve the thousands of people living there. The houses, simple in exterior are luxurious inside.

Chandeliers, rich rugs and silken wall hangings combined with the latest TV sets and karaoke stations. Invited for a meal, we would all sit on the rugs as dish upon dish would be placed in front of us, delicious and beautifully presented.

When there was a wedding on the Water Village, they had a great system.

Maybe six families with sons and daughters around the same age and living in close proximity, would organise the wedding. They would share the cost and the work, allotting the beef preparation to the best beef cook, the fish to the best fish cook, and so on for chicken, vegetables and rice.

Then the chosen cooks chose their helpers to do the less important work.

At the end of the meal, after the last drop of rose syrup, water, fruit and cakes had been consumed, the dishes were removed to the decking.

It was so impressive. The women beautifully clad, sat cross-legged on the decking, with water hoses, then enormous basins of soapy water,. followed by more hosing to rinse and stack out to dry in the ever- present sunshine.

I haven't mentioned the numbers. I asked about how many people they gave invitations to.

"We send out maybe six hundred, then multiply it by three."

When I attend a Western wedding, all elegant hats and invitation cards with RSVP, I feel nostalgic for the community weddings with everyone helping. When the mosque prayers were sung, they held their hands in prayer and then got on with the work. So natural and beautiful a sight.

The golden topped mosque, down river, and the Sultan's palace with flying golden turrets up river. I saw every day.

The view from the water taxi, the golden roofs, the wooden buildings and walkways is the sight that stays with me of these happy years on the island of Borneo. As I write and glance up at the small watercolour of the mosque and the Water Village, I think it was the heart of Brunei.

In contrast the splendour of the palaces, the fountains, indoors and out, marble and gilt. Palm trees, like giant fans, bordering the long twisting lit up by thousands of lights to the entrance. Four thousand people assembled in their uniforms, or national dress or evening wear, the women wearing white for formal evening wear, unlike our code and black for morning wear. It was the occasion of the Sultan's birthday.

As I watched the two queens standing by the Sultan, I realised that I would never see such magnificent diamonds again in my life. They shone like blue fire, emitting so much light. Entrancing to watch the tiaras sparkle!

I had put a flower in my hair, a hibiscus. I was admiring my neighbour's beautiful orchid and I commented that mine seemed to be drooping a bit.

She laughed, as she told me that hibiscus flowers close at six pm.

Two experiences were going on separately here. Life in the capital, Bandar Seri Begawan, and life in the jungle.

I was fortunate to have an Iban friend who introduced me to her culture.

Animists in the main, living in longhouses, individual homes connected by a long roof and adjacent meeting hall which ran the length of all of the houses. Twelve houses was a small long house. Over thirty was quite common, we went on treks in the jungle, balancing on logs, falling off and into the mud. After the first half a dozen times it was really fun realizing we all looked like rugby players at the end of a game, covered from head to toe in mud and leaves and leeches!

The Gawai ceremony is the end of one season and the beginning of the next. Harvesting the rice is very important and blessing the fields to bring good luck to the people is a major part of the culture.

I watched the elderly shaman, long white hair, striding down the meeting hall, striking at each end with his staff, a bit like Gandalf. I whispered to my friend,'But he looks like a Native American Indian.'

'Yes', she replied, 'we come from the same root. One branch of our ancestors came from Central Asia and went overland via Greenland to Canada and North America and the other branch by sea to Borneo and that is why the Canadian Government awards three scholarships a year to us, their' cousins.'

The shaman's cloak, the three feathers in his hair, the longhouse tradition, the beadwork, the family totem animal (crocodile, turtle, monkey etc.) the weaving of the myths and legends, no written language, it all made sense. But, I thought, why do we not study Anthropology in schools instead of battles. It would be so much more relevant. Perhaps then we would understand each other's culture better.

And in the process, find ourselves too.

In the other life in the capital there was the 'Hash,' Ladies had one too. A paper hunt through the jungle. Not for me but did it once.

Never again! Running through the dense jungle, birds nest plants catching the hair, strange noises and the poor soul who had laid the trail had thrown at her not by me, imitating the men's hash. Really!

Tuak, the ceremonial rice wine is drunk at these ceremonies. I have a recipe but truthfully, don't feel I am entitled to make it.

So lucky to have had these experiences. I missed, for a long time, the sound of gibbone shattering in the trees, the sudden dramatic sunsets and the people.

Once a large monkey sat on the roof of the car looking into the house, then shinned up a tree hunting for birds' eggs. Another time, a tree frog, bright green, jumped on to my face and clung with its sticky pads when I was shooing it away from the cats. The same blessed cats that came from Scotland to Germany and then to Brunei. Their coats adjusted to being thick and furry instead of shedding, as we had expected. They hunted in the jungle, adapted brilliantly. till they died off in their early twenties. When they flew from Germany we were messaged to say they were held up for a short time between flights. I had this lovely notion of them sitting in First Class, paws crossed with a cigar and a gin and tonic at the ready!

Brunei was a hub in a way for Asia. India could be easily reached from there. Bali also. Singapore was about two hours away.

I made my plans to experience as much as I could. I began the first tour in Borneo seeing Sarawak and Indonesia, then onto the mainland of Malaysia then. Singapore and by bus up to Thailand which was beautiful, with its huge Buddha statues by moonlight. The return journey, stopping in Johore Bahru was one of the worst experiences.

I checked in to the medium priced hotel and went to my room, turned off the light and then switched it on again. The floor was alive with cockroaches so many crawling over each other. In a panic I phoned reception and told them there were cockroaches everywhere and I'd have to change rooms.

'Madam, they are in all the rooms. Don't worry, just leave the lights on. They don't like light. They will go back to the bathroom drain.'

There were hundreds of rooms in that hotel. I slept with the lights on, my clothes on, on top of the bed, with my suitcase tightly closed.

I am sure there are many good hotels in Johore Bahru, just that was my luck!

My next tour was to the Cameron Highlands in Malaysia to cool down from the heat of Brunei. Clothes had to be changed three times a day and the moist heat made drying them difficult. And there I came across a Buddhist temple where a very holy monk had lived and died and his skull was crystal. It was called the Diamond temple.

There are wonderful garden centres in the Highlands full of geraniums, lilies and begonias all colours of the rainbow, pastels and vibrant magnetic colours.

I fell in love with a red, red, red lily which they told me was an Amaryllis.

I asked to buy a corm. They said it would not grow in Brunei. That it had to be above sea level. I argued until they agreed, paid my sixty ringgit and as soon as I was back in Brunei, planted it in a huge pot by my front door.

Months went by, nothing. Three years went by, nothing

THEN, one morning I looked down and there was a strong column of green. I swear I could almost see it growing as I watched. Each morning inches more.

Then the burst of outrageously red blooms, huge lilies. It wasn't only me who was affected. Cars were stopping and people were asking what is was and could they, please have a corm.

Synchronicity at work. At this time a new baby was born to the family. My older son got a good job in Japan and my son in law got his PhD. in Archaeology. Coincidence? No such thing!

Aubergine in Coconut Milk

At the palace function I have already described, there was a food I could not identify. I asked the Indian lady with the orchid in her hair what it was.

'Very easy to make.' So it is.

SLICE THE AUBERGINES ABOUT HALF A CENTIMETRE THICK WITH SKINS LEFT ON

2 TABLESPOONS OF VEGETABLE OIL
1 TABLE SPOON OF CURRY POWDER OR TO TASTE
1 TIN OF COCONUT MILK OR CREAM WITH A LITTLE WATER

Instructions:

1. FRY THE CURRY POWDER IN THE OIL
2. ADD THE AUBERGINE SLICES

3. KEEP TURNING, WHEN JUST COOKED, ADD THE COCONUT CREAM
4. SEASON WITH A LITTLE SALT IF REQUIRED.
5. SERVE WITH RICE

Fish in Satay Sauce, Kampong Ayer

WATER VILLAGE
GINGER, GARLIC, SPRING ONIONS, CUCUMBER
SLICED
PEANUTS LIQUIDIZED WITH WATER
CINNAMON
PACKAGE OF MIXED SPICES, CLOVES STAR
FLOWERS
COOKING OIL
CHILLIES
FISH GRILLED

Instructions:

COOK ALL THE INGREDIENTS EXCEPT THE
FISH TOGETHER

TO MAKE A RICH SATAY SAUCE

SERVE WITH THE GRILLED FISH AND RICE

I WATCHED THE COOKS MAKE THIS WITH
NO MEASUREMENT.

We shared recipes from each others' culture. What fun
we had!

INDIA

India was a major influence in my life although I did not live there, my dream was to visit. Brunei made it possible, not too long a flight

I asked my friends who had been there, where they would advise me to visit. They were so enthusiastic in helping me plan my trip round India by train, second class.

One month prior, a water buffalo came out of the shadows and hit the jeep head on. It went lumbering off, crying piteously, a lowing cry, into the jungle. The jeep was written off. A vertebrae in my neck was broken so I was wearing a collar when I got to India.

My route was planned : arrive in what then was Madras, one centimetre on the map should take two or three days by train, go down to Cochin, carry on up the west coast seeing My sore, Hyderabad, Puna, Aurangebad.

Then visit Rajastan, Jaipur then Delhi, Agra, the Taj Mahal and then up to Manali. There was no travel agent helping, just a map. The night of arrival in Madras overwhelmed me. There were hundreds of people at the airport and I realised the vastness of the undertaking. My pilgrimage to India suddenly seemed like a mountain to climb. As I lay in bed in a hotel which the taxi driver had recommended, (probably owned by a relative, with a spin off for him,) I saw a mass of light gather on the wall and Lord

Ganesh face appeared before me and he said,

"Do not worry, I will carry you on my back round India."

He had the most compassionate eyes. So then I knew I would be all right.

I still took sensible precautions, up very early to make the most of the day and back before darkness fell, knowing it was unusual for a western woman to travel alone. It was choice. Friends and family wanted to accompany me and share the adventure, but this was a pilgrimage. When it is a compromise,

'Where shall we meet? Where is the coffee shop?' etc the energy is different, and I knew that if I were in a temple and might want to stay for a long time absorbing the atmosphere and pray, it could be irritating for others.

As I am writing this, I am realizing for the first time, that I was doing then, what other people now, would call a retreat. The difference being a retreat is in one place, one centre, usually with one guru. My "retreat' was India.

I visited Trivandrum in the south, watching the unusual fishing technique of the fishermen, felt the terrific heat and saw the lushness of the land.

Cochin, Kerala was a very emotional experience for me. I was walking along the street of spices and was told that Jews had travelled and settled at the time of Nebuchadnezzar, king of Babylon, 605 BC – 562BC, Old

Testament. Thousands of years ago and been there in Cochin ever since.

There were synagogues, stars of David, seven branched candle sticks, and now, as then, I am overwhelmed by such a testimony of faith.

To have kept the Faith for thousands of year. in a huge subcontinent of different faiths, Hinduism, Buddhism, Jainism, Sikhism and Christianity moves me to tears. The courage and enduring faith, like a light that is never extinguished.

There must be a past life for me in some way to feel such an affinity with this place.

Just went to William Blake's poem' And did these feet in ancient times'

He would have felt the same, I am sure!

And now to modern times! On a ferry spoke to a lovely young Indian girl studying engineering. She told me that Kerala has almost one hundred per cent literacy and the top students are directed into the professions like Science and Engineering and only then, are the Arts considered.

Meeting great people on the way was a joy, as watching the traditional dance of Kerala, Kathakali, sacred of course to the goddess.

It was quite hard on the body, travelling by train to these destinations.

But pilgrimages are not meant to be comfortable. The slatted wooden seats of the second class carriages were made more comfortable by sitting on the neck brace!

Once, travelling through the night, there were six bunks and I was relegated to the top bunk by a formidable Indian lady who took the bottom one. My bunk faced a Sikh gentleman and I was pretending to be asleep as he unwound his turban. I travelled throughout my times in India in Punjabi dress, a tunic and loose cotton pants. Better for blending in.

There were problems on the way. A car breaking down on the road to a Temple south of Mysore, in the blazing sun, miles from nowhere, with only one bottle of water for the six of us, mine! And they were Australians and Indians who should have known better. Being spiritual doesn't mean giving up on common sense. Sharing the water on the way and sharing the oranges on the return bus journey, because they didn't think of buying them from the little shop for a five hour bus journey. That did annoy me and I was ill for days with dehydration and sunstroke.

That was bad, feeling helpless and vulnerable on my own.

A kind hearted waiter kept bringing me, unasked, sweet lassis, to get me well. A young guy, devout Hindu, who would make puja, prayers, by the river, on his day off. I was so grateful for his kindness to a stranger. India is a spiritual country. It is tangible as soon as you step off the plane.

At New Delhi I was struck by the eye colour of the guide at the entrance to the Red Fort. Instead of shades of brown, they were piercing grey with a dark rim round the iris. I was reminded of the eye colour of the people of Portland near Weymouth in UK and the people of the Himalyas who have the same eye colouring, blue, grey, hazel and green with a dark rim.

The Taj Mahal was exquisite, the burial place for Mumtadsa; a young Iranian girl who enchanted Shah Jahan as he rode back through the Zanskar Valley from the Middle East.,

She was his favourite wife. She was a seer, and her dreams from the angelic Realm, showed her both the

Taj Mahal and the Shalimar gardens in Srinigar, beside Lake Dal, Heart Lake.

She described the visions she saw and her husband carried them out in the material world.

Such a testament of beauty and love and yet he bankrupted India in its making. He brought mosaic artists from Italy and the best sculptors in marble and on her tomb, the perfect diamond, the Koh iNoor, the stone of her wedding ring, worn on her toe which was the custom.

As the moonlight shone on the diamond, her face was irradiated with light. The Shalimar Gardens followed exactly the proportions of the vision. Given, perfect symmetry and wonderful flowers and plants.

As I felt in Washingon on the way to see the Hope diamond, the proportions there are perfect, following the Golden Ratio, the same harmony and satisfaction of the senses were in the gardens.

I travelled First Class from Delhi to Agra. I thought the Taj Mahal deserved nothing less. (And I replaced the support collar round my neck).

It was smaller than I had imagined but glowed almost opalescent in the morning light. A photographer told me it appeared different throughout the day. When I saw the place where Lord Elgin had prised off the Koh I Noor from the tomb to send it to Queen Victoria along, no doubt, with the Elgin Marbles from the Parthenon in Athens, I felt ashamed of his behaviour.

In the First Class compartment with padded seats and chai being delivered through the window, an incredible voice was singing. A rich baritone. The voice was more beautiful than any I have heard. The singer was legless, on a trolley. With tears streaming down my face I passed as many rupees as I could find and turned to look out of the window.

Deliberate amputation for the purpose of begging as a livelihood hopefully does not happen any more in India.

That is India, a constant paradox of beauty and pain. There is the white Taj, a river behind, and a lake in front for a perfect mirror reflection.

Shah Jahan then proceeded to build the black Taj beyond a bend in the river but Aurangzeb, his son, stopped the building and had his father imprisoned, but still able to see the Taj Mahal. Aurangzeb was exactly the opposite of his father. He memorized the Koran and the payment for this was just enough to buy a headstone which is very simple, white with an orange and green border. The people had suffered enough.

My next visit to India, during the same year, was to visit the Golden Temple of Amritsar. Actually, that one had had an effect on my imagination more than seeing the Taj Mahal. Maybe because it was a temple with healing powers in the moat. A sacred place to Sikhs.

Wherever I go in the world and there is a problem, if a Sikh is there, they help. So I have a high regard for their faith.

'By their actions you shall know them.' (One of my favourite sayings.)

First you think, then you speak, then you act.

I flew into Delhi, pondering whether to go to Kashmir for there had been Unrest between Pakistan and India, but I met an Indian friend at a bookstall and asked his opinion. He said straight off.

"You will be safe. You will love the cool, fragrant air, the scent of the roses, the herbs and the wildflowers and they need tourists badly for tourism was their main income. They are property rich and cash poor. Go and help them."

I arranged to be picked up after the Golden Temple of Amritsar by Rashid who would meet me at Simla and take me across the lake to the houseboat.

It was a long journey to Amritsar and I had no water left. As soon as I arrived a driver picked me up in his tuk tuk straight to the Temple. No opportunity to buy water. The energy was amazing and it impressed me more than the Taj Mahal less beautiful, but more vibrant. It was busy! Every visitor is fed, some rice, some lentils a few raisins. And when the sun goes down even if an enemy were to come, he would be treated as a guest, fed and allowed to rest.

Being dehydrated and prone to migraine attacks I had to stay in an hotel. Overnight till the worst passed. The owner who practised Ayurvedic healing cut a lemon in half and rubbed my temples. It would have worked earlier but this was the crisis.

Next day I resumed the journey to Simla, hoping that Rashid would be there though it was a day late. As I got out of the bus, some hours later, a young man approached me.

He was tall, wearing the cloak that all Kashmiri men wear, picked up my suitcase and nodded as I asked if he was Rashid. We got onto the skiff that would take us to his houseboat. Half way across the lake another boat appeared with a guy standing up, balancing, as he held up a large sign with my name and passport number printed in huge letters.

'It is I, Rashid,' he called. So the two men rowed like mad to a houseboat which was apparently, Sultan's.

It was a dilemma. What should I do? So told them the only fair way was to toss a coin for it, They agreed, Sultan sullenly.

'Heads,' Rashid called and so it was.

As Sultan pulled away, he said, "The rich always win!" Certainly wasn't referring to me!

Rashid made no fuss about the kidnapping of his client and shook

Sultan's hand before he left, saying, 'These are hard times for everyone.' The houseboat was beautifully carved. I had the whole boat to myself! Before, when tourists came, it would be lucky to get one room at an exorbitant price.

It was very cold at that time of the year so we huddled near the stove in the centre of the main room. I was given a kangris, a clay pot with hot charcoal inside. It was a form of central heating, for you sat cross legged and draped the cloak over the kangi. A great invention for the climate!

I ordered one of the cloaks, grey with a red lining. It kept me very warm and was made in less than a day.

Rashid showed me the log of all those who had visited. from 1920.

I asked who 'Chuck 'was that they kept thanking.

"My father, the name they gave him."

I saw the Shalimar gardens as we punted around the lake then walked round them, a bit neglected but still beautiful. That was the first of my visits to the Himalyas and a project was planned

For my nest visit, to climb in the Himalyas. It was an exciting prospect and I thought about footwear. I tried on various boots when I was in UK. All so heavy on the feet, so decided on gym shoes or plimsolls.

The time came and I was back in Simla beside Lake Dal. I loved to look at the Floating gardens. Over time, roots of water lilies had been gathered and bound

Together to form islands. Soil was then put on top and vegetables were planted like lettuce cabbage and onions. Again, a brilliant use of the environment.

Rashid, his sister, nephews and parents lived in a small house at the side of the lake. Food for me was cooked there. Simple food obviously and the younger boy would join me. When I asked him would he like biscuits, His shy reply was, 'Might there be butter and jam on them?'

Food was scarce but that young boy, no more than eight years old, kept the family with his fishing skills.

I asked him how he did it. 'I look at the lake for maybe twenty minutes until I see a fish. Then I cast the line.' On one occasion they had to catch him for the fish was so big. It was pulling him in.

The time came for our expedition it was about a three hour drive to our starting point in the foothills. There were the pony men waiting for us maybe three or four, strong men in their cloaks. I was in jeans, shirt and pullover, gym shoes on my feet. When I looked at the mountains, my heart sank. The immensity of them was terrifying.

We pitched camp and that night I had a warning dream Rashid told the men and all agreed we needed to give a gift to the river that flowed at the foot. I had to throw bread in and say prayers to Lord Shiva. His temple was on our way.

The pony was surefooted and we climbed to 15.000 feet. And made camp. There was a kind of shepherd's bothy and the men gathered round with their Kangris under their cloaks, telling stories of the mountains and catching up with local gossip. I felt stupid in my dressing gown.

However when we had arrived men came out with rifles Rashid was friendly calling them his brothers. I thought they were poachers, but apparently not. They were freedom fighters, holed up in the mountains. The pony men had descended leaving two ponies behind.

The next morning Rashid and I left the bothy and began our climb on foot. We had to leave early for the avalanches began at 2 pm. It was hard breathing and we were only carrying our ice picks.

I looked over my shoulder and saw my late father emerge from beside the river below. He had taught my sister and I to climb in the hills, so as the three of us climbed, me in the middle, Rashid to my left and my father to the right.

We crossed the snow bridge, each of us slipping and using the icepicks to catch each other. The pass that we had started from. was the Zanskar and Honza valleys meeting. It was a wonderful sensation of peace, the world left far behind. The things we saw. The Valley of Kings, the faces in the rocks.

The figure of an angel or fairy in the clouds, the mushrooms that magically appeared as we climbed. The fossilized shell that blew me away. And my father's voice,

'Carry your own weight! Put your feet at an angle as I taught you!'

We knew we were being watched and both said it at the same time.

In the snow in front of me was a large footprint, deeper at the back than the front. with four toes in a line and one at the back, bigger, somehow grown or falanged from the others. We both knew he was shy, the Yeti. I took my camera out to photograph him and put it away again. Why disturb his peace in the holiness of the mountains.

Rashid said he had never had a day like it and he had been climbing from age seven with his father. I think we were given an incredible blessing from the mountains. We had climbed two thousand, five hundred feet from the camp so in all seventeen thousand five hundred feet.

Time was important to get down to camp before 2 pm and just as we got there, my father disappearing near the river again, there was a rumble like thunder and the avalanche began. Snow cascading down, remorselessly.

We had been speaking very quietly on our way down.

We gathered up our stuff from the camp, and suddenly we were surrounded by the men of the previous night.

Rashid spoke in a friendly manner, wishing them well. Some had idealistic faces. Some had not. Rifles in their hands, by their sides.

We got on the ponies, Rashid saluting and myself, looking at each one in the eye. Felt my back prickle for I didn't know if they would shoot me.

We didn't speak a lot on the way down. The pony men met us at base camp to pick up the ponies and we got into the car. The way we had come was closed The bridge had been blown up.

The following day, Rashid didn't bring breakfast, his sister came. For three days he was bedridden. I asked if I could visit him.

He said simply, "I would have died for you, Dolphin." Their nickname for me. I believe that is the truth.

So now here I am, writing at my desk in Cyprus, asking myself Why did I do that?

A longing to be on the roof of the world?

To set myself a target?

To prove something to myself?

To manifest in the material world what I was doing in the spiritual?

Probably a bit of all of these.

That was the peak experience I have had in my life, No pun intended!

Sometimes electronics delete and repeat I am leaving this duplication. Maybe the guides are telling me something! The duplication has now disappeared.

Kashmiri Potatoes

BOIL POTATOES TILL FIRM. DICE THEM.
INTO 1 INCH CUBES
TOSS IN BUTTER AND CHOPPED FRESH
MINT.
FRY TILL GOLDEN BROWN

Sweet Lassi

NATURAL YOGURT UNFLAVOURED
ADD WATER
HONEY
CHOPPED FRUIT LIKE MANGO
WHIZ

Savoury Lassi

NATURAL YOGURT
ADD WATER
1 CLOVE GARLIC CHOPPED
1 SPRING ONION CHOPPED
PINCH OF SEA SALT
WHIZ

CYPRUS

This is a truly beautiful island. When I return from abroad, I wind down the window of the car and say, "I love you Cyprus!" It is a diverse island, of blue, blue sea, rugged mountains, lemon trees, olive trees, grape vines and red geraniums everywhere. There are small, typically Mediterranean villages scattered over the island. Summers are roasting hot, over 40 degrees, and winter, when I am writing now, is cold in the morning and after 3 pm usually pleasant between these times.

It is very popular as a tourist destination. Beds are fully booked in the hotels every year. I came here with a work permit to teach with the British Military in Episcopi, from Brunei. After such a warm country, always sunny, living in the sun felt right. My four children were in agreement. We had looked at France, Spain, Greece and Cyprus was the unanimous choice.

I had been told by a very spiritually advanced friend, Cypriot, that my home would be in the mountain area above Paphos. He described it exactly I had looked at fourteen areas and properties and when I saw the view I knew it was here. So many Fated experiences took me here.

The church is very powerful, Greek Orthodox, and there are churches, large and small everywhere. Kykkos monastery is the best known, richly ornamented with gilt icons of outstanding beauty.

Religious artists who paint the icons of the saints have to study a course in Theology before they are permitted to paint sacred art. World Heritage churches are found in Troodos Mountains. They have the most wonderful icons, kept safely in the mountains. These churches are characterized by the wooden roofs, almost Swiss in appearance.

They are very steep because of the heavy snows that fall in Troodos in Winter. The tradition in Cyprus is for flat roofed houses.

Archangel Michael's church is very special to me and I am sure to many others. He communicates very clearly there.

At the other end of the island at Pomos, there is a church which is believed to heal people miraculously and spontaneously. The whole area feels healing as the sea is behind the church and there is a beautiful rose tree in the grounds. Only six of these grow in the island usually beside a church. The flowers look like roses, a lovely pink.

There is always perfumed air, of jasmine and thyme and in April or May. The Damask roses bloom and the perfume is intoxicating.

Agros, the village of roses, is the centre for the perfume making, the rose face creams and lotions, rose water, rose ice cream and a variety of other products.

I wanted to plant a cherry tree on my small field which has fruit trees. Oranges, lemons, almonds, apples, olives and of course there is the vine over the pergola. However this village is not of a sufficient altitude for a cherry tree to grow.

When the house was being built there was a small lemon tree where the patio would be and the builders wanted to remove it. I refused and they built the patio around it. It gives wonderful shade and lemons. The gardener will prune it next week. in the middle of February. What a powerful, strong tree it is, like a protector.

Cyprus was given as a gift to Cleopatra from Mark Antony because it was seen as a jewel of an island with its fertile land and trees which could be used for building ships.

The emperor Constantine built many ships so even more trees disappeared. His mother, Saint Helena, asked her son to bring cats to Cyprus to rid the island of snakes. He sent a shipload from Egypt and one from Asia and so the population of cats to this day on the island, show these characteristics.

My Cypriot cats, Cadmus and Core came from the Monastery of Cats run by a small community of nuns. It was a delight to see the colony of cats spread out luxuriously on benches, walls, walkways and trees fed on yogurt and cheese, the nuns make themselves. Both tabby cats. The nun handed me Cadmus said, 'male', and picked up another scrawny one, and said, "one for company."

Well Cadmus escaped one night and a few weeks later, kittens were born.

She responded now to a male name so I didn't rename her. She sadly died of a snake bite. Core got all the loving attention then, but three years later, she died of old age. Both are buried under an olive tree.

Now there is an ever changing pride of cats who live in the field, the patio, on. the garden chairs, fed by the gardener in my absence.

One, Little Kit, and I have a strong affinity. I took her to the vet and had her speyed, fed her and kept her company for three days as she healed. She is very loving, till she is not!

Cyprus predates Ancient Greece and almost every week, new Archaeological treasures are discovered. It was the centre of the most iconic cult in Ancient times. Ships would sail into the harbour and processions of people would walk along the sacred gardens to the temple of the goddess Aphrodite. She was deified in her form of a conical rock which her priestesses would anoint with perfumed olive oil. Kings, queens, emperors would come to ask for her intercession.

One of the most well known views is the birthplace of Aphrodite, or Venus, as the Romans named her. There is a sacred triangle between that spot, Amathus near Limassol, and Heracleion, the most ancient port of Egypt.

Greek Mythology lives on in the names of the people. Aphrodite, Paris, Elena after Helen of Troy, Heracles, Menelaos, Orpheus, and of course the very common names, after saints, Angelos, Andreas, Georgiou and Michailides.

As Brunei was a hub for my travels in South East Asia and India, Cyprus is the hub for Dubai, Europe, Greece even Singapore and then on to Australia.

It is unique culturally, the language spoken here is the language of Homer, and would be understood with difficulty in Athens.

I know I have been here in another lifetime as an Egyptian official. I. sailed into Egypt the first time I visited and knew it was a familiar journey.

That sense of familiarity has never left me. The energy is healing.

And everyone feels at home soon as they land.

All my Cypriot friends are great cooks. They were all taught by their grandmothers and they have shared with me. How lucky I am!

Of course wonderful vegetables and fruits grow abundantly, so everything is fresh. In an Italian cookery class the amazing chef explained that in Italy the paternal grandmothers taught the grandsons to cook, while the maternal grandmothers taught the granddaughters to embroider and make lace which the men then sold abroad. Very similar here in Cyprus. Perhaps when the

Italians invaded, they brought their artistic gifts with them from Venice.

The Knights Templar were here also and Limassol was the centre for sugar refining. There is such a wealth of history here!

In the following recipe STIFADO, I tried six different methods till I found the best. In one, only vinegar was used. In the next, only white wine was used. In the next, red wine was used. In the next lemon. In the next mushrooms so here is the ultimate Stifado! Only beef or hare are used.

Stifado

FRY 10 ONIONS IN OIL(,ANY KIND). TILL GOLDEN BROWN.
PUT THE ONIONS ASIDE

BROWN THE CUBES OF BEEF IN THE OIL FROM THE ONIONS
ADD WATER, STOCK CUBE (IF YOU WISH) OR SALT PEPPER

1 HEAPED TEASPOONFULOF CINNAMON POWDER
COOK TILL TENDER. ADD MORE WATER IF NEEDED.

ADD 1 SMALL GLASSOF WHITE VINEGAR
AND 1 GLASS OF RED WINE
REDUCE.

ADD COOKED ONIONS.

SERVE WITH POTATOES OR RICE

It was a kind taverna owner who took pity on me when I told her how often I had tried for the best stifado She told me the combination of vinegar and wine made it perfect.

Aubergine Dip 1

CUT THE TAIL OFF THE AUBERGINES CUT IN HALF

LENGTHWISE, NO NEED FOR OIL

PLACE UNDER THE GRILL ONCE OR TWICE TURNING, TO OTHER SIDE TILL SOFT

SCOOP OUT THE FLESH AND CUT UP THE SKIN.

PUT INTO BLENDER

2 CLOVES OF GARLIC CHOPPED FINELY
1 TABLESPOON FUL OF TAXINI
ADD OLIVE OIL AND LEMON JUICE IN EQUAL QUANTITIES OR VINEGAR INSTEAD ON LEMON JUICE
SALT AND BLACK PEPPER

BLEND TILL CREAMY. SERVE WITH PITTA BREAD.

I MAKE THIS WITH SKINS, GIVES A SMOKY
FLAVOUR.

If I had to choose which1 food I would want to live on
for the rest of my life, it would be that dip! But boring
eventually, only one food!

Aubergine Dip 2

SLICE AUBERGINES IN HALF LENGTHWISE

GRILL BARBECUE OR ROAST IN OVEN

SCOOP OUT THE FLESH

PUT INTO BLENDER

ADD GROUND ALMONDS OR WALNUTS
1 CLOVE GARLIC
CHILLI POWDER OR SWEET PAPRIKA
SEA SALT
OLIVE OIL EQUAL MEASUREMENT WITH
LEMON JUICE OR POMEGRANATE JUICE

BLEND. SPREAD ON A PLATE AND PRESS
THE BACK OF A

TABLESPOON INTO THE MIXTURE TO MAKE
A PRETTY FLOWER.

I use almonds and sweet pakrika but love chilli as well!

The countries following are all flowing from the hub, Cyprus. From Cyprus, over the years, life branched out to include Australia, Singapore, Malaysia, China, Hong Kong, Japan, Egypt, Skyros(Greece,)Dubai, USA, Ireland and UK. They were all by invitation and I was happy to be a Light worker in each country, sharing the gifts of healing, seeing and teaching and meeting wonderful healers, dedicated people, on the way.

Australia, the land of birds, where I dream every night when I visit.

Singapore, a peaceful haven with fascinating temples.

Malaysia, palm groves everywhere and the best food in the world,

Penang, an island to the north where the hawkers create gourmet food.

China, so vast and Shanghai which I visited twice a year, a fascinating city.

Hong Kong with its wonderful approach, the Nine Dragons.

Japan, unforgettable seascape, mist over the horizon and an eagle hovering,

Timeless.

Egypt, mysterious and regal, Nile its heart centre.

Skyros, island of winds and legends

Dubai, architecturally amazing and so many diverse cultures.

USA the sound of the trains and their lonely hooting across the plains.

Ireland, its soft green energy and other wordliness.

UK, history in every city, town and village.

What a glorious world we live in in its natural state. It is our responsibility to try and keep it so.

In conclusion, in Troodos mountains there are cherry trees and it is a paradise when the trees are in bloom in the orchards.

When the fruit appears, red, vibrant and juicy, they are made in traditional recipes, as liqueurs, cherry brandy, cherries in syrup, cherry jam and other delicacies.

The delicate pale pink or white blossom against a blue, spring sky must be a forerunner of Heaven.

So, enjoy the cherries on the cake of your life, wherever you are,

Keeping life simple, and sharing!

Printed in the United States
By Bookmasters